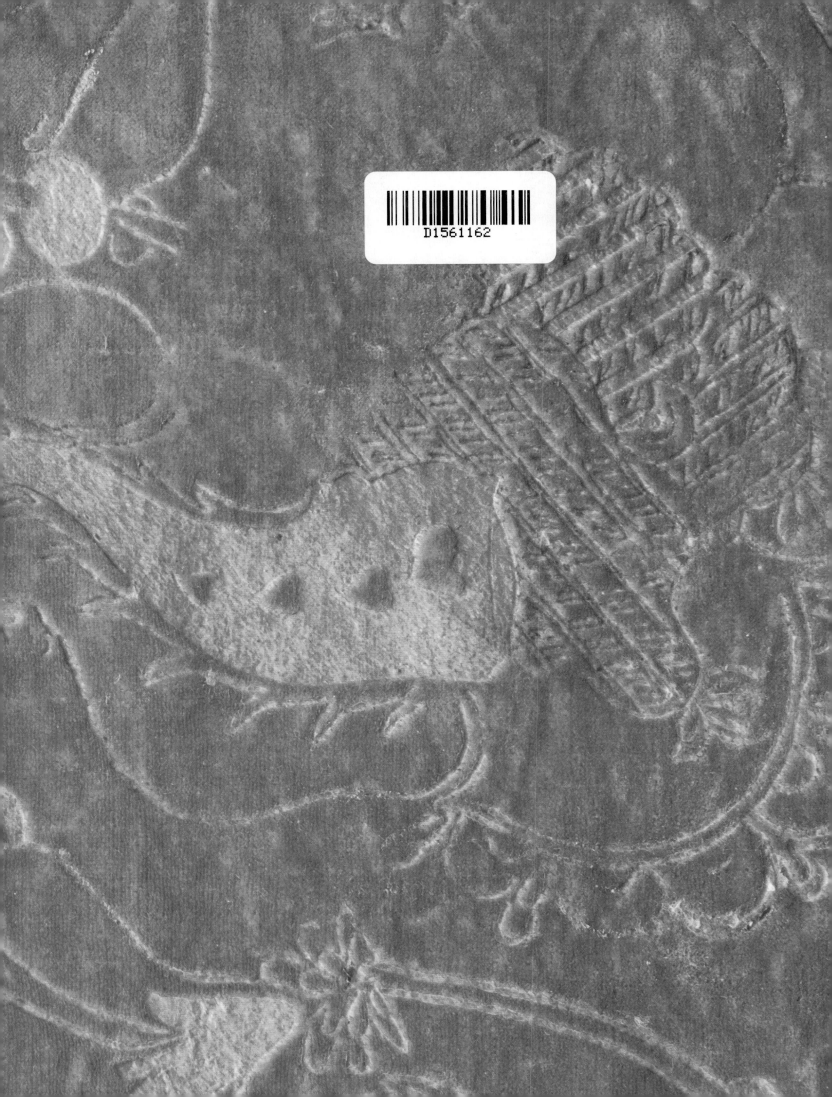

AMELIA HANDEGAN

Rooms

Amelia Handegan with Ingrid Abramovitch

PRINCIPAL PHOTOGRAPHY BY PIETER ESTERSOHN

RIZZOLI
NEW YORK

New York · Paris · London · Milan

With love and gratitude to family, friends, and coworkers who provided unselfish support when I didn't necessarily deserve it. Thank you also to my clients, without whom my ideas would have remained unfulfilled visions. I want to especially thank my father, who sent me off to England to select my first container of antiques; my mother, who gave me her strength and taught me to draw a camellia; and my husband, who takes me to faraway lands and helps me to finish my sentences.

amelia

Page 2: **Silver-handled Indian fly whisks hang on either side of an eighteenth-century English portrait in a hallway. A Jamaican server, circa 1840, holds a silver tea service.**
Opposite: **Camellia Japonica.**

Contents

Introduction

One of my clients would frequently question my reasons for choosing a specific color palette or certain furnishings or textiles for his home. Eventually, he stopped asking. "Get back to me after you put on your swami hat," he started saying, "because I know you can't explain it."

I confess to always having been more of a visually connected person as opposed to a verbal one. I gravitate toward understatement in the interiors that I design. I love quiet rooms—where the windows are dressed only if needed, color is distributed in careful and even doses, and the furniture is edited. If a room has fine proportions and light, its interior furnishings won't have to work so hard to make that room beautiful. Such places need only a few wonderful pieces—a sofa to sink into, interesting antiques, or personal collections of art and accessories that feel authentic to its owners.

If I hesitate to provide my clients with a road map, it is because I believe that an interior should evolve during the process of learning about the structure of the home itself. The unique qualities of a space should play a role in dictating what will take place

there. The architecture, location, and the owner's own aspirations will gradually come together to reveal a plan. An interior designer can, of course, bring his or her own taste and experience to the project, but to be successful the design of a home has to be based on much more than a decorator's inspiration: it should be built on a creative layering of a space's construction, history, and, perhaps most importantly, how it holds light.

With over thirty years of experience in interior design, I may not have entirely overcome my reticence to explain myself to every client, but I have come to realize that I do have stories to tell. I have worked on a huge variety of projects, including the preservation of many eighteenth- and nineteenth-century houses in my home base of Charleston, where I find the historic architecture endlessly fascinating. Elsewhere in the South, my commissions have ranged from restaurant interiors, including the design of Charleston's Peninsula Grill, to the decoration of a cabin in the Blue Ridge Mountains to an equestrian center in Florida and the preservation of an almost two-hundred-year-old plantation house in rural Virginia. Interior design work has taken me

Page 6: Light reflects off gold silk curtains in a sunlit dressing room at the William Gibbes House. The nineteenth-century dressing table is French and the armchair is from amelia, inc.

Opposite: **Paprika red curtains set off the grisaille scenic wallpaper in the dining room at Rose Hill.**

out of town, with projects, to name a few, in such places as Maine, the Virgin Islands, and Wyoming. I've decorated homes old and new and large and small, and I've also lived in a variety of spaces. One thing I know for sure: Color, or the absence of color, is of primary importance. Even a slight change of hue can make a difference in creating a sense of harmony in a room.

I grew up on a farm in South Carolina that was a grant from King George III, which has been in my father's family since the eighteenth century. When I was young, we grew soybeans, cotton, wheat, and corn and raised cattle. I spent my childhood in the farmhouse that was built by my grandparents when they married. My father still lives there.

My best memories are of Saturdays, when I would be dropped off at the home of Miss Corey for my art lessons. Evelyn Corey was a watercolor artist who lived with her sister. She gave classes in painting and ceramics while her sister furnished cookies. We sculpted clay in a converted chicken coop, but I loved watercolor art the best. Miss Corey would say, "Amelia, do you see that tree? Let's paint it." I'd get the grays and browns but she would say, "Don't you see the purple in the bark?" She taught me to look deeply and to see the world in full spectrum.

My early interest in decorating was nurtured by our nanny, Rosalee Brown. She was a gifted storyteller and I loved being with her. We would pretend to furnish houses with images from catalogs and magazines. Rosalee would select the basics and I would focus on the decoration and the fluff.

When I realized I was not going to be a studio art candidate in college (despite my early success at Miss Corey's), my major changed to art history. A trip to Europe at eighteen changed my focus to interior design and architecture. After receiving a degree in art history, I enrolled in design school where I studied with San Topol , who has since become a great friend. Stan was acquainted with the iconic decorator Billy Baldwin who had designed homes for Jacqueline Kennedy Onassis and Diana Vreeland. Stan brought a few of us to New York in the mid-1970s to open our eyes to what was happening in the design world. I'll never forget it.

We were invited to Billy Baldwin's studio apartment for cocktails. It was a chic cocoon with walls in dark brown lacquer, and lined with book-filled brass étagères, like those he designed for Cole Porter's library. From there, Stan took us to the spectacular apartment overlooking the East River that Billy had designed for the advertising legend Mary Wells Lawrence. I was transfixed by the fusion of traditional and contemporary elements: antique furniture and oil paintings coexisting happily alongside blue-striped rugs and Baldwin's low-slung slipper chairs.

It's commonplace today but the marriage of old and new was fairly radical at the time. Baldwin's interiors felt absolutely modern and fresh yet were rooted in traditional design, both in his classic approach to room arrangements and his embrace of such Old World elements as upholstery and antiques. His rooms revealed to me that you don't have to reject the past in order to create spaces that work in the present. Since then, the designers I have admired—from the late Albert Hadley to the amazing Belgian antiquarian Axel Vervoordt—have been fearless in embracing this mix of new and old, side by side.

Perhaps it is my background in art history, but I tend to conceptualize space like a painting. Often, I start with a wall color. I tend to gravitate toward unusual shades that are somewhat hard to name or distinguish: grays that go purple, pink with a gold undertone, greens that have more yellow than blue, and browns that range from chocolate to tobacco. Starting with an unusual hue, I frequently box myself into a corner. The challenge is in finding a way out—a dab of this color and that one, a pink pillow to contrast with a green wall—until the whole house feels balanced and comes alive. By the time it's finished, a home might have as many as thirty variations of color, yet at first glance it will seem to consist of only two or three.

I have a passion for travel and the cultures that I discover are a constant source of inspiration. I always come home with a new palette in mind. In 2012, my husband and I made a trip to the Kingdom of Bhutan, tucked away in the Himalayas. The temples there are decorated in beautiful hues of pink, yellow, blue, and the saffron of Buddhist monks' robes.

On a trip to Ireland, hiking through the countryside past an old graveyard, I noticed a corroded fence. "That's a familiar blue," I told John. The fence was painted that particular color you often see in the South Carolina Lowcountry. We call it "Haint Blue." "Haint" means a haunted spirit, and that shade of blue has always been used to keep the ghosts away. I've used it on my own exteriors in Charleston and Folly Beach.

Whenever I travel, I look for combinations of colors that may not work at all on paper, but have somehow come together because a person with a great eye, or out of sheer necessity, has assembled disparate elements with astonishing results. Examples abound in central India, where the sense of color is vibrant and totally unpredictable. Being there inspired me to combine deep reds with purple and pink with gold. I try for that same sense of spontaneity in the rooms that I design. Just as a composer might play with counter harmonies in a musical composition, I'll deliberately pick a hue that doesn't match the others just to upset the balance and create a bit of a surprise. I think this is often the key to creating a space that appears to have evolved slowly, over time, instead of feeling as though it was stamped from a pattern book.

One of my first clients, a woman in her seventies, had a beautiful old house in a town near Charleston. It had Fortuny fabric on the dining room walls, which I thought was very beautiful. I tried to talk her into completing her bedroom in chinoiserie blue and white. "I'm going to give you some advice," she told me. "Don't over decorate. It won't look good." She was right. Anybody can cover everything in blue and white. I've done it, and it's often attractive, but to me, the best result looks collected and assembled over time.

It has been said that the first rule of decoration is that you can break almost all the rules. I think this is true, but only after you have learned and practiced those rules. Light, color, texture, and great materials make a room. Sometimes, a beautiful bed with a red sari across it, a dark painted floor, and one great painting on the wall is enough. Sometimes, what is omitted speaks louder than what remains.

After living in my 1820s Charleston double house for over twenty years, I recently moved to an apartment. A few months ago, I was poking around an antiques shop downtown when I noticed a pair of Moghul-inspired obelisks from northern India. They looked familiar and then it hit me: I had seen a pair like them almost forty years ago in Mary Wells Lawrence's apartment in New York, the one that had been furnished by Billy Baldwin. The dealer confirmed that they had indeed come from Mrs. Lawrence's home. They now frame the fireplace in my living room, reminding me of that trip to New York and reinforcing my view that great style is timeless.

Right: **The living room of a Church Street house in Charleston glows in its palette of warm apricot. A seventeenth-century portrait is framed by curtains in raw amber silk. The coffee table has a top in antiqued mirror and is by amelia, inc. The circa-1840 stools are American.** *Following page:* **In a living room, furniture and objects were carefully selected for scale, from the painting of a dress by Todd Murphy, which is perfectly framed by the wall's moldings, to the nineteenth-century Viennese hall chair whose back ends just below the chair rail. The curtains are in blue silk and the amelia, inc. chair is topped by an Aubusson cushion.**

The Houses

Birdseye

A Lowcountry
Revival Style House

I am a big fan of using murals in the interior design of a home. One of the most ancient of art forms, mural painting often incorporates the architectural elements of a space into its imagery. A mural can transform a challenging span of wall, enliven a room with awkward proportions, or set the tone for a color palette. Best of all, an illustrated wall or ceiling can be a source of constant delight. Mural painting is a vanishing art form, but it shouldn't be.

At Birdsong, the interior architecture called out for a mural that would establish the house's place in its surroundings. This recently constructed, inspiring structure is located on a broad bluff overlooking Bohicket Sound on Wadmalaw Island in South Carolina. The home has the generous proportions and details of a historic place. It was designed by the Charleston preservation architect Glenn Keyes in the Greek Revival style, complete with white columns and a porch overlooking the wooded grounds that slope down to a wide river.

The owners divide their time between Charleston and this home and working farm. Inspired by the design of a Georgia house dating before the Civil War, the owners asked Keyes to replicate its cruciform plan, calling for two intersecting hallways that are twelve feet wide. These crossed corridors create four square corner rooms, each with thirteen-foot ceilings, on a single floor. Massive interior hallways receive the pulse and flow of the house. While the overall footprint is not huge, the home's classical scale creates a sense of grandeur irrespective of square footage.

Having previously worked on the interior design of the couple's home in Charleston, I was asked to help with the decoration of the farmhouse. Since the wide hallways were such a prominent feature of the design, we incorporated them into the living space. For instance, there is no dining room. Instead, informal meals are taken in the spacious kitchen, while more formal dinners are served in the long halls where tables are temporarily set up for these special occasions. The transverse hallway terminates in a writer's room at the bedroom end and, at the other, a pair of great doors lead out to a broad, comfortable porch with views of giant oaks and the water beyond.

Opposite: **The entry hall has a custom scenic mural by Scott Waterman.**

Above: **The farmhouse on Wadmalaw Island, just south of Charleston.**

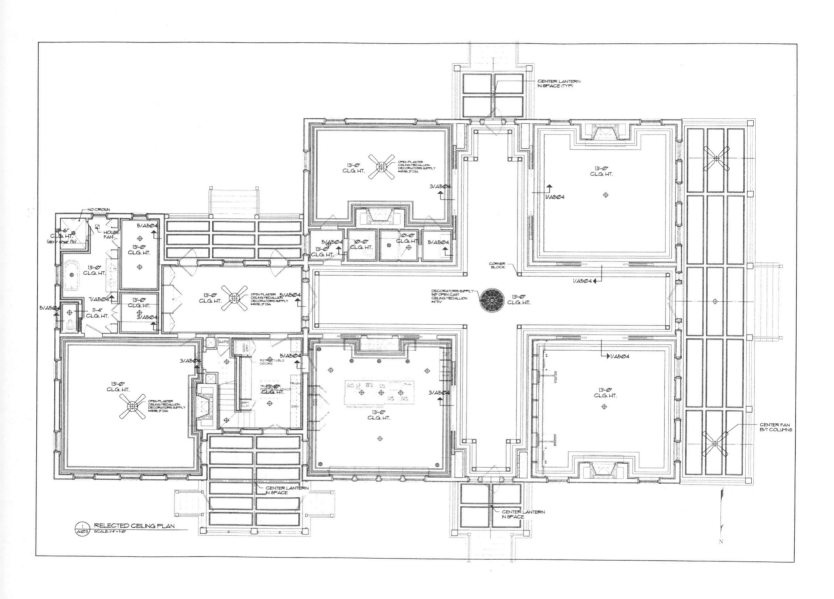

Above: **The floor plan was designed around two intersecting hallways, creating four square rooms at the corners.**
Right: **An Italian Neoclassical Revival chandelier hangs in the entry.**

Following spread: **The living room is lively in Farrow & Ball Print Room Yellow, with a mix of formal and informal elements. The windows are dressed in sheer linen by Sabina Fay Braxton. The mantel was designed by the home's architect, Glenn Keyes.**

The rooms we call the "corners" include a sitting room, a library, the kitchen, and a bedroom. I opted for strong Farrow & Ball colors against the muted shades of the mural for the living room, library, and kitchen. The period architecture combined with the rural setting demanded a careful balance between dressy and dressed-down elements. The sitting room, with its antiques and oil paintings, feels less formal with its jute rug and sheer linen curtains.

My favorite flourish remains the delicate hallway murals painted by Scott Waterman of Los Angeles. Done in the style of the 1920s Charleston watercolorist Alice Ravenel Huger Smith, each mural depicts the view outside its walls. Murals are a classic way of bringing natural elements to an otherwise refined setting. To commission one requires courage and no small degree of trust in the skill and sensibility of a good painter, but when well conceived and executed, a mural can infuse a dose of the extraordinary into daily life. Birdsong is such a place.

Previous spread: In the library, the custom walnut desk has a leather top. The antique bronze chandelier is Dutch. *Right:* The kitchen, in Farrow & Ball Orangery, has an early-nineteenth-century Swedish trestle table and a custom light fixture.

Right: In the hallway, a large nineteenth-century English convex mirror hangs above a linen press from the West Indies. The chairs are English Regency. *Following spread:* The bedroom has a calming palette of soft cream and watery blue.

28

Fish and Goat

A Barrier Island Retreat

Folly Beach is just a dozen miles from downtown Charleston but feels a world apart. This barrier island is called the "Edge of America," not only for its positioning out in the Atlantic Ocean, but also because of its perennially bohemian atmosphere. When we were young, my parents cautioned me to stay away from Folly Beach. Once a magnet for pirates, the island later having served as a garrison for the Union Army in its repeated attempts to capture Charleston during the Civil War, Folly has always attracted all manner of renegades, artists, writers, and, of course, surfers, given its claim of having the best waves on the East Coast. This island with its beautiful sunsets is one of my favorite places. Even with its offbeat bars and aging hipsters, it still manages to remain family friendly. It's a destination where kids can play safely and walk to the beach.

The housing stock of Folly Beach is historically unassuming, from its one-room fishing cabins to its midcentury bungalows on pilings. A few years ago, my husband, John, and I caught the bug and bought a circa-1950 beach house clad in asbestos shingles, having the appearance of a cereal box on stilts. Our plan was to renovate the old 950-square-feet house, while joining it with a new two-story bedroom addition. I enlisted the help of two talented friends, Dan Sweeney of Stumphouse Architecture + Design and Glenn Keyes of Glenn Keyes Architects. Dan perfected a challenging flat-roof design for the new addition, which contains four bedrooms and four baths, and added a cupola that we use as a home office. Glenn created a temple-like screened porch and a U-shaped entry stairwell that tucks up and away behind a hedge of bamboo.

On the old house, we replaced the asbestos shingles with shiplap boards stained dark brown. For the new structure, those boards continue on the first story, but above them we used corrugated metal sheets running vertically up to a parapet wall, which is accented by a crowning strip of that familiar Lowcountry blue. The vivid color (which mysteriously changes hue depending on weather conditions) tells visitors that they've arrived.

Opposite: **Our screened porch looks directly onto the Atlantic. This indoor/outdoor space has custom sofas made from marine-grade plywood and a pair of George Nelson cigar wall sconces.**

Above: **The beachfront bungalow on Folly Beach, South Carolina.**

The old house became our central living space. We removed the sheetrock walls that had formerly divided it into tiny rooms and demolished the low ceiling in order to expose the roof rafters. This makes the space airy and bright. An L-shaped layout now contains a whitewashed living and dining area that flows into the sunny kitchen. To make the interior a bit more special, the rafters are reached by six-inch pine boards laid horizontally throughout.

White felt right in this beach house, but I am not the sort to go totally minimalist. I enjoyed furnishing the place with a broad range of collected items of diverse origin.

These objects include beds from Colonial Virginia and India, a Jamaican mahogany cupboard used as a bar, a blue Swedish chest in a guest room, and rugs from just about everywhere including a pair of Navajo saddle blankets perfect for the master bath. The seaside under-porch on the ground floor has an old painted swing from India known as a *jhula*, and a cypress-paneled guest room has a Persian tribal rug.

The place is pretty nice when it is in order, but we try to never forget that it's a beach house out on Folly.

Opposite: **The kitchen, which retains its original pine floors from the 1940s, is painted white. The cabinetry is by SieMatic and the striped rug is Bolivian.**

Above: **The dining area has an antique Swedish table and vintage iron chairs.**

Above and opposite: **The living room has a custom amelia, inc. sectional and a vintage kilim rug.**

Previous pages: **A circa-1880 Jamaican kitchen cabinet is paired with an Asian stool (page 40). In a hallway, a painted floor in stripes and lozenges (page 41).**

Above: **Remnants of groins, man-made structures once used to stop beach erosion, form a graphic pattern in the Atlantic Ocean.**
Opposite: **Blue-and-white pattern play in a guest bedroom.**

Above: A pair of vintage Jantzen swimsuit mannequins frames a custom round mirror on a stair landing.

Opposite: An eighteenth-century French portrait hangs over an antique blue Swedish chest in the guest bedroom. I commissioned a local artist, Robert Shelton, to paint a bathing suit and Chanel glasses onto the portrait for fun.

Previous spread: The master bedroom is quietly
dramatic in white and red. An antique bed from Virginia
is covered in a quilt made of vintage Indian fabric.
The side tables are skirted with mirrored wedding
quilts from India.

Above: In a guest bathroom, a silvered bowl from
Turkey was converted into a sink basin.
Opposite: A guest bedroom has walls lined in natural
cypress without a finish.

Above: **A breezeway frames the view of sand dunes on Folly Beach.**

Opposite: **Reclaimed shutters painted in Haint Blue are used as shower doors. The painted swing is from India.**

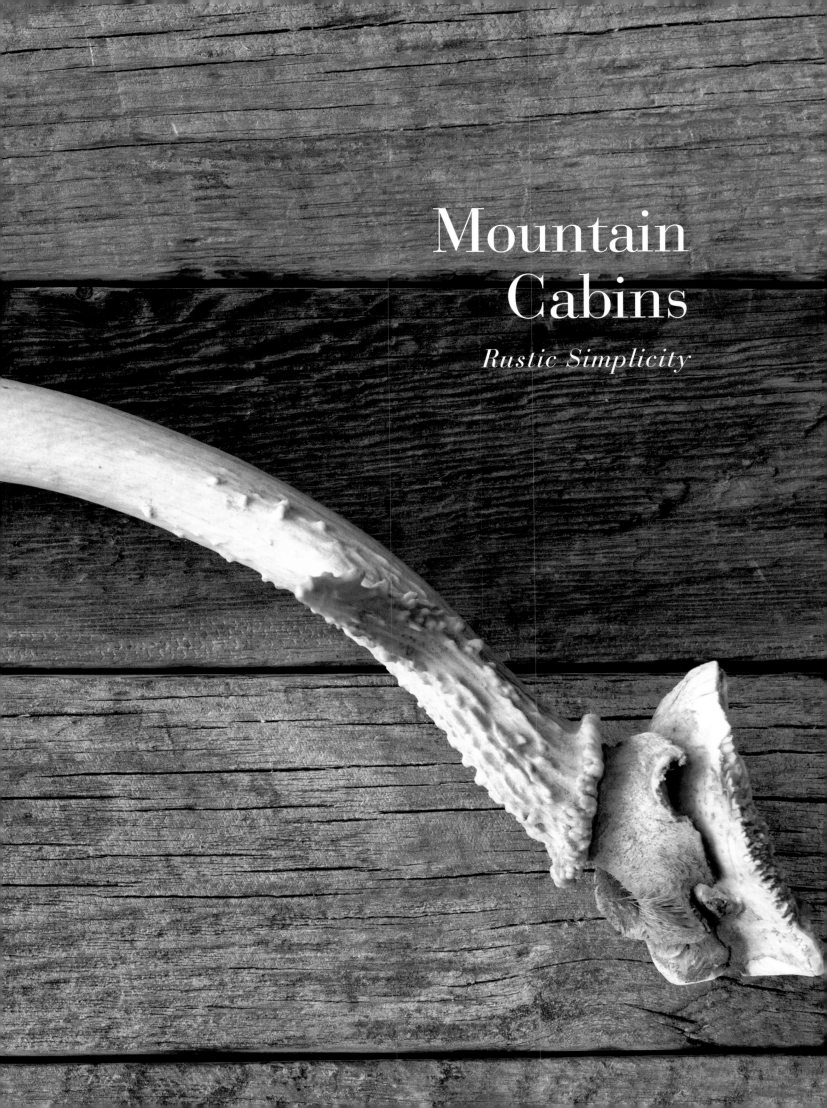

Mountain
Cabins

Rustic Simplicity

With its pine-tree-covered mountains and cool forests of ferns and mosses, North Carolina's Blue Ridge has long provided lowland Southerners with a welcome refuge in summer. A Charleston family purchased seventy-five acres of wooded land near the town of Cashiers for their retreat. To anchor the central building plan, they transported three antique cabins from Pennsylvania of less than one thousand square feet each. Tim Greene, a local architect, used two of the cabins to form the main house and guest quarters, while adding twig porch railings and bark siding on the gable ends. The third cabin was transformed into a master suite, linked to the main house by a covered breezeway.

The homeowners had clearly trusted in the rustic elements, so for me there was no point in trying to compete with the weathered beauty of the natural construction. When it came to interior finishes, I decided to run with the same approach. We added reclaimed barn boards to the ceilings in the kitchen. The state-of-the-art appliances, cupboards, and drawers were hidden behind paneling made from those same boards, which were decades old with traces of original paint. In the master bedroom, with its stone fireplace and unfinished wall and ceiling, we selected antique French floorboards, to be face nailed. Here was a place to be sparing with color and focus instead on texture. When I did add color (such as the punch of orange on the inside of the living room's double doors), I specified glossy paint, which created contrast against the patina of the wooden surfaces.

With this rugged backdrop in place, I finally got to play in selecting the furniture and decorative objects. White, with accents of saffron, coral, and red, dominates the living room. Rather than place a sofa in front of the stone fireplace, we circled four white armchairs around a low wooden coffee table on an antique carpet in rust and gold. A vibrant red contemporary canvas by Haidee Becker, placed atop the unfinished wooden mantel, seems to evoke a campfire in a room that still feels only a step removed from the wilderness outside.

The quirky architecture compelled creative design solutions. Our goal was not to waste an inch of those cabins' interior spaces. In the guest loft, we fashioned a row of curtained bunks inspired by old

Opposite: **The master bedroom porch is furnished with a vintage iron daybed that has been fitted with an old-fashioned-style ticking mattress. The outdoor seating includes vintage Lloyd Loom wicker chairs and an Asian elm side table.**

Above: **An antique cabin from Pennsylvania was one of three transported to North Carolina's Blue Ridge Mountains to create a rustic retreat for a family from Charleston.**

Above: In the common room, four custom-upholstered club chairs in white form a conversation circle in front of the stone fireplace. A vintage Oushak carpet echoes the red and orange in the large contemporary painting by Haidee Becker. An antique antler chandelier hangs from the room's soaring wood ceiling.

Opposite: The dining room's antique German trestle table has a weathered appearance that melds with the room's timbered walls. The lacquered black finish of a set of antique Chinese elm country chairs provides contrast.

Above: **The fronts of the kitchen cabinets were made from reclaimed barn boards and fitted with iron strap hinges. They conceal everything from storage to modern appliances.**

Opposite: **A Moroccan chest serves as a console.**

railway sleeper compartments. One of my favorite features is the curtain rod, resembling a long tree branch. Space was also tight in the master bathroom so rather than block natural light the solution was to float a mirrored cabinet in front of the windows. Below it, an old pine cabinet was converted into a sink.

The home's timbered backdrop seemed to enhance just about any interesting piece. Discovering this gave me the chance to decorate from divergent sources, with materials that might have seemed in wild conflict in a more traditional home. For the dining room, we found a set of Chinese country chairs in dark elm to surround a nineteenth-century English trestle table. In the master bedroom, vintage French leather club chairs face a new campaign-style canopy bed topped with white mosquito netting. In the bedroom's private porch, we placed old wicker chairs and an iron daybed. When one is there, surrounded by dappled light and the sounds of the mountain forest, there is a sudden desire for a midafternoon nap.

Right: **In the master bedroom, an iron canopy-style bed has a lace-trimmed white coverlet and a canopy in mosquito netting. A pair of antique French leather chairs flanks the stone fireplace.**

Above: **The master bath's vanity was fashioned out of a vintage pine cabinet. An antique mirrored cabinet was hung in front of a window.**

Opposite: **The smooth finish of the white cast-iron bathtub contrasts with the rough-hewn walls. An old wood-toothed rake is used to hang towels.**

Above: A guest bedroom is furnished with a four-poster bed in hickory and split cane. An antique wool area rug is layered on top of a cotton twill rug to add pattern and texture.

Opposite: The en-suite guest bathroom has a rustic mule chest converted into a vanity, as well as a "tramp art" mirror. The bench is vintage French rattan.

Above: **A ceramic bar sink sits on top of a cabinet made from boards with their original red barn paint.**

Opposite: **In the sleeping loft, a row of beds was fitted under the sloping roof. Hemp curtains hang from a tree-branch rod, affording privacy.**

Island Home

*A Colorful
Turn-of-the-Century Cottage*

The setting of this island home is Sullivan's Island—a historic barrier island north of Charleston Harbor and a former haunt of Edgar Allan Poe's. Sullivan's has no hotels, only private homes and old stone forts. Many homeowners live here full time, drawn to the white sand beaches and the opportunity for relative seclusion in close proximity to the city.

This project illustrates the general principle that color sets the tone. Here, a family with two school-aged children asked me to create a relaxed and child-friendly environment, while infusing as many adult grace notes as possible. By the time I was invited to work on the interior, Charleston architect Beau Clowney had undertaken a revision of the classic 1890 Lowcountry house. He retained much of the original façade, including the wraparound porch and the tall shuttered windows, but the updating had doubled the structure in size. The renovation had a lot of charm, with sunny rooms and pine plank walls, ceilings, and floors. My goal was to keep the atmosphere cheerful without making it feel too much like a summer cottage since it was to serve as a principal residence.

A common misconception holds that the best way to enliven any space is with a can of paint. That approach may represent the only practical or affordable solution in some circumstances but in this house my strategy was to work within a neutral color envelope that complimented the old pine walls and floors throughout the house. I then introduced color away from the walls. Later, doses of color were applied to the walls as a leitmotif, repeating and reemerging in layers from room to room in response to factors ranging from the light to the color of textiles and window treatments.

Fine art often provides the spark to ignite a palette. In this case, the encaustic triptych by Timothy McDowell installed in the entry hall turned out to be a gold mine. The paintings depict an imaginary landscape rendered in lush and dramatic hues. I was especially drawn to the broad spectrum of orange. It was those shades that helped to create a color story, with drama intensifying or ebbing throughout the house.

The soft coral of an Oushak carpet balances the triptych. The small sitting area near the entry is full-on orange with its tangerine sofa and matching 1940s slipper chairs. This narrative continues from room to room, from the bright carrot of Hans J. Wegner's

Opposite: **The front porch ceiling has remnants of the original light green paint.**
Above: **The 1890 house on Sullivan's Island, South Carolina, was doubled in size.**

Following spread: **The entry foyer sets the color tone for the home's palette.**

Above: In the wood-paneled foyer, an Oushak rug picks up shades of red and coral that appear throughout the house.

Opposite: A sitting area's bold tangerine sofa finds visual balance when paired with cerulean cushions and a pair of skirted chairs in natural linen.

Wishbone chairs in the kitchen to the soft apricot of the languid figures in the dining room's mural, inspired by Matisse's 1952 cut-out masterpiece, *The Swimming Pool.*

While the overall ambiance is colorful and warm, the surprising fact is that most of the home's color palette consists of neutrals. This is demonstrated in the living room's cream walls, its white duck slipcovered sofas, and the floor-to-ceiling gray of the kitchen and breakfast room. This pared-down scheme, in combination with the streamlined linen-covered furniture, provides the home with a relaxed contemporary feeling. Orange gives it energy.

Above: **A modern chandelier of glass and steel hangs over the dining room table, a custom piece with a hand-planed wood top over an iron base.**

Opposite: **The mural in the dining room was inspired by Matisse's *The Swimming Pool.***

Above: The home's warm palette reappears in the breakfast room in the form of a set of orange Hans J. Wegner Wishbone chairs. The natural linen sheer café curtains also have orange trim.

Opposite: In a high-ceilinged living area, the pine-paneled walls are contrasted with a white-slipcovered sofa, a striped cotton carpet, and white curtains. A custom Parsons table in yellow lacquer provides a sunny pop of color.

1820s
Greek Revival

A Country House in the City

For over two decades, an 1820s house in Charleston was my home. Located on what was once waterfront property on the Ashley River, this Greek Revival home is a classic example of a Charleston double, meaning that it is two rooms wide with a spacious central foyer. With its whitewashed cypress boards and red metal roof, it feels like an old Southern plantation house set high off the ground in the middle of the city. When I purchased the house, the shutters had a crescent moon motif and were painted a vibrant blue. I left them this color as they reminded me of Haint Blue, that classic South Carolina shade that stands out so well against white.

When I moved in, my youngest son rode a tricycle in the entrance hall and my older son was away at boarding school. In what seems like a minute I was an empty nester. As the years passed, my travels took me to such places as Laos, Cambodia, and India. Each time I came home inspired and with suitcases stuffed with exotica, most of which found its way into my house. In recent years, I've come to appreciate a more pared-back approach to furnishings but I still have a soft spot for new discoveries, especially beautiful textiles.

With no client to please other than myself, I indulged my preference for the colors in the fan deck that are often overlooked. I chose cantaloupe for the family room and bronze for the dining room. The kitchen was painted a brown gray that I call Pluff Mud, after the sediment found in Lowcountry marshes and tidal flats. These shape-shifting, off-kilter colors are often a challenge to work with. What pleases me is exploiting color relationships and balance in order to provide depth of tone.

Gradually, I turned my attention to updating the baths and kitchen, which had last been renovated in the 1950s. The floor plan did not have an inch to spare so those rooms had to remain relatively modest. The kitchen had been moved years before to the first floor, incorporating the porch that once wrapped around the house. I added antique pine floors, simple white cabinets, and counters

Opposite: **In the entry hall, a painting of Cuba from the 1940s hangs over an Italian eighteenth-century bench with a rush seat.**

Above: **The 1820s Charleston double house where I lived for over two decades.**

and oversized subway tiles in a coordinating marble. The large window stayed intact and a breakfast area was created.

Meanwhile, on the ground floor, where the original kitchen was once located, I found a warren of rooms including two with dirt floors. I turned one room into a guest bedroom. Another became a bathroom with closets and a large porcelain freestanding tub. In both those rooms, I retained a wall of original brick, while the other three were covered in beadboard. The other two rooms remained storage areas, albeit with new floors and beadboard walls. One of those spaces had been the original kitchen and still has a massive brick fireplace, which was once used for cooking.

The house has perfect classical proportions, including tall ceilings and square rooms with lots of wall space. It could have been furnished in a traditional manner, but with my inclination for the unusual, I challenged myself to place my offbeat collectibles in rooms that were probably entitled to things more subdued and elegant. The end result was a house that felt comfortable and suited to my needs without sacrificing the integrity of the original floor plan.

Right: **The drawing room has tall ceilings and classical proportions. I took an eclectic approach to the furnishings, combining an eighteenth-century Italian chandelier with a Napoleon chair and an antique French mirror. The slipper chairs, which I designed, along with the paper lantern shades on the carved peacock floor lamps, add a contemporary note. The custom velvet sofa has a scallop-shaped back.**

Previous spread and above: The dining room's bronze wall color is typical of my preference for unusual and slightly off-kilter hues. A British Colonial dining table was surrounded by a set of Anglo-Indian Colonial rosewood armchairs. A local antiques dealer created the chandelier by adding crystal arms to a trunk of repurposed metal fronds. An 1840s Jamaican sideboard holds a silver set in the dining room. The portrait above it was painted in Charleston in the eighteenth century.

Opposite: In the breakfast area, Regency chairs were updated with velvet seats in a jaguar print. The circa-1860 pedestal table and antique serving trolley are Jamaican. The contemporary paintings are portraits that I commissioned of my ancestors from Michael Roberts.

Right: In the master bedroom, an American four-poster bed, circa 1840, is silhouetted against walls painted a warm cream. A Twigs reproduction of the classic scenic wallpaper, The Monuments of Paris, was turned into a screen, which backs an American 1840s chest and an English églomisé mirror.

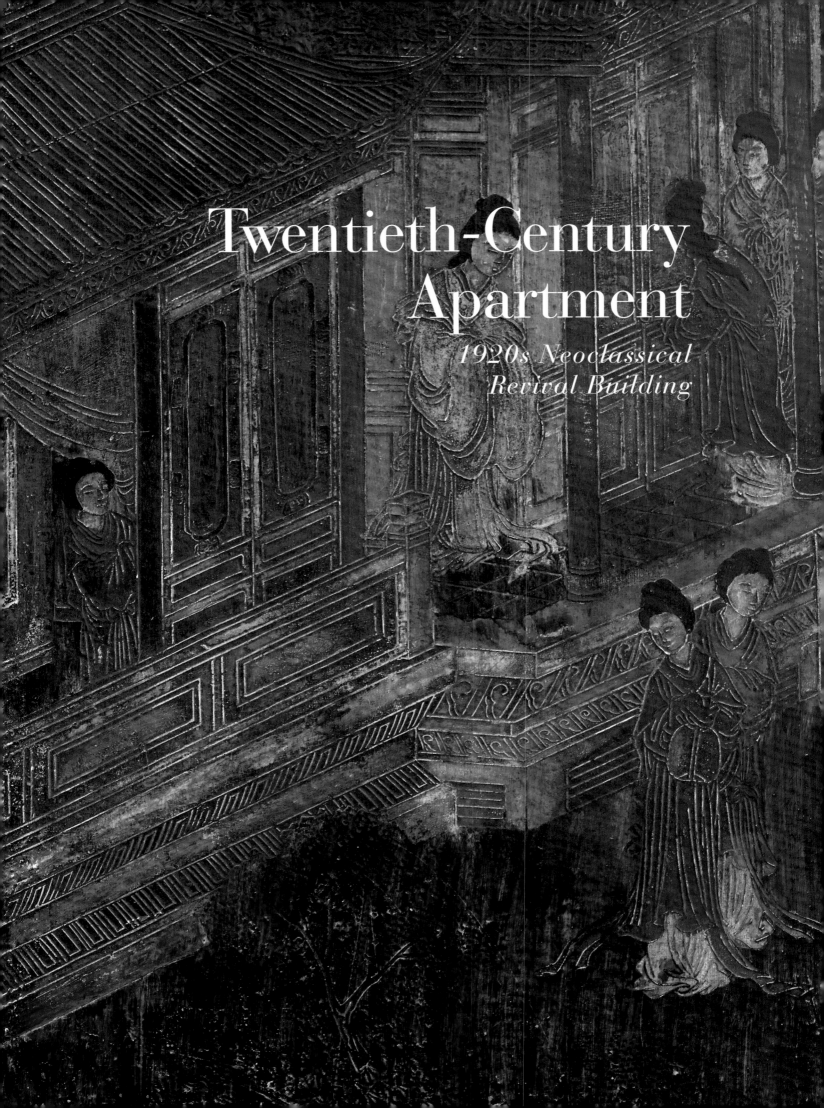

Twentieth-Century Apartment

*1920s Neoclassical
Revival Building*

Three years ago, I sold the house where I had lived for more than twenty years and downsized to an apartment close to Charleston Harbor. Built in 1923, the Neoclassical Revival structure had formerly housed a vocational school and earned a preservation award for its meticulous restoration. The apartment—one of seventeen in the three-story building—had high ceilings and tall steel windows. After considering these credentials, along with the picturesque location, I found the place irresistible.

While the exterior façade was preserved, the interior of the old school was new. Without any historic elements to save, I was free to reconfigure the interior walls. Since I typically work within the confines of a historic structure, here was a rare opportunity to draw my own floor plan and dictate the flow of the living areas.

In the entry, I added a barrel-vaulted ceiling and storage hidden behind doors with painted panels based on a favorite Japanese textile. My motivation throughout was to stay minimalist. This quiet approach grew out of the loftlike scale of the rooms, with their thirteen-foot ceilings, and the prewar industrial feeling that the huge glass-and-steel windows evoked. To that end, I disposed of the traditional crown molding, simplified the baseboards, and put the emphasis on refining the apartment's materials. Ho-hum stone floors were replaced with marble and textured wood. Walls were redone in a neutral Venetian plaster with an undertone of Dutch Pink, that favorite of mine that lends a subtle glow in the evening light.

After living so long in a house filled with furniture, a sparse interior seemed refreshing. I tried to pare down my personal inventory to a minimum, keeping only those items I couldn't bear to part with, although I probably kept more than I should have.

Some of my favorite spaces in the apartment were created anew. To bring light in, I separated the large existing master bedroom into two: a smaller bed chamber and a new gallery hall with a glass-and-steel door that leads to a private courtyard. Folding doors lacquered in a bronze gold open onto the bedroom. This color theme accelerates into a blaze of gold, yellow, and blue in the Pichwai painting we found in Rajasthan that now dominates the gallery wall.

Opposite: **In the entry, the brown-and-white diamond-pattern marble floor is reflected in a distressed mirrored wall. A Buddha rests on an eighteenth-century console.**

Above: **A sofa's pillows are in handmade fabrics by Sabina Fay Braxton in a palette of olive, gray, and berry.**

Above: **A coromandel screen hangs over a Ju Mu wood console. A pair of antique bronze vases is filled with fresh magnolia leaves. The chinoiserie box was purchased in England on my first buying trip. The two gilt lamas were found in India.**

Opposite: **In the living room, Venetian plaster creates a neutral textured backdrop for antiques and colorful textiles. The portrait above the mantel was painted in Charleston in 1756. The furnishings include a pair of bergères by amelia, inc., a Swedish circa-1820 sofa, and an Italian chandelier.**

My husband, the cook, needed light for the kitchen and we decided it had to move. The existing one was situated in a windowless space in the center of the floor plan. Kitchens tend to be a daily focal point for us, so I repositioned it into what was a bright third bedroom. The result is now full-on modern, with charcoal gray lacquered cabinets and a breakfast

area furnished with an 1840s Jamaican trolley and a marble-topped antique table.

What to do with the windowless former kitchen? The solution was to create an interior library. I lined the walls in olive hemp and painted the bookcases to match. The color looks striking when offset by

Above: **The living room's steel windows are dressed in sheer alpaca shades.**

Opposite: **In the corner, a banquette in bronze-green velvet serves as a dining area. An English Regency table is in rosewood with boulle work marquetry.**

the hallway's panels, which are Dutch Pink with a pattern inspired by Indian *jali* screens. A custom-made wall-to-wall sofa in weathered blue velvet now infuses the space with hushed comfort. To me, a wall of books is simply beautiful, imparting a relaxed ease unrivaled by almost anything else.

Above: The kitchen has contemporary cabinetry, made by SieMatic, in charcoal lacquer and stainless steel. The floral-etched bell lanterns were custom made in India.
Opposite: A gray wall in the breakfast area is hung with a range of artworks by Alfred Hutty, Elizabeth White, and Mario Robinson. The large painting is by Chuck Bowdish. The Jamaican trolley and antique table came out of the kitchen in my former house in Charleston.
Following spread: The former kitchen became an interior sitting room and library. The walls are hung gallery-style with an eclectic collection of portraits. The custom blue velvet sofa and red lacquer table are from amelia, inc. A pair of midcentury slipper chairs is covered in a gold fabric by Christopher Hyland.

Above and page 106: The American poster bed, which came out of my Greek Revival house, is now fitted with an antique Fortuny panel behind the headboard and a Dauphne hand-blocked fabric canopy. The bed's small pillow is made from an antique Indian bolster cover. The gray lacquer side tables are from amelia, inc. The lamps are made from Tibetan horns. The gilt Garuda mask holds an antique Fortuny fabric.

Opposite and page 107: In the rear hallway, chartreuse-gold silk curtains frame the large custom steel doors that open onto the garden. A large antique Pichwai depicting Krishna, from the Nathdwara school, frames an Anglo-Indian desk. The doors to the bedroom are in lacquered bronze.

The George Eveleigh House

A 1740s Georgian

Even in Charleston, the George Eveleigh House is a remarkable structure. Built in 1743 by an Indian trader, the two-story brick house is an architectural survivor, both inside and out. The property, which includes a main and carriage house, boasts some of the finest early Georgian interior and exterior detailing in the city, including a piazza with the original Dutch terra-cotta pavers.

The interior of this unique house demonstrates that reclaiming a period house need not result in a reenactment of the past. Here, Christopher Liberatos of the New York architectural firm Fairfax & Sammons, together with Richard Marks, Charleston's go-to contractor for historical buildings, collaborated on a masterful restoration that preserved the original architecture while adding functional, contemporary features such as a modern kitchen and bathrooms. With the renovation in such capable hands, I had the good fortune to begin the interiors in a house beautiful in its emptiness.

The eighteenth-century asymmetrical floor plan, one of the few that remains in Charleston, consists of a first floor with an off-center entry, a morning room, dining room, kitchen, and a long drawing room on the second level with four windows and a door opening onto the front piazza. There is also a former kitchen house that serves as guest quarters.

Having purchased and preserved a piece of history, my clients wanted an interior that would quietly complement the unique architecture. The wife, who owns an art gallery, envisioned rooms where her collection would be in harmony with the Georgian woodwork. But at the same time, she did not want her selection of artwork to be restricted by the period architecture. To keep the house from feeling dark, I chose a warm palette of pale colors. Often, I softened the tones with an umber glaze, which further enhanced the shadow lines of the Georgian paneling.

In the small entry, we lined the walls with an apricot silk to catch the limited light that comes through the windows and transom. On the same floor, the dining room is in a subtle melon glazed with a light sienna in order to, once again, enhance the shadow effect of the paneling. Adjacent to that striking hue, the butler's pantry called out for something special,

Opposite: **The piazza of the house is lined in terra-cotta Dutch pavers, an eighteenth-century feature.**

Above: **The George Eveleigh House was built in 1743 and is a fine example inside and out of the Georgian style.**

so we covered the walls in a Gracie wallpaper where white and off-white foliage grows against a background of tobacco brown.

By contrast, the morning room is paler and more ethereal. With its cream-colored wall paneling and muted upholstery, the space is deceptively spare. It is filled with such luxurious details as gilt valances and textiles in silk, velvet, and wool. But the furnishings, including a pair of midcentury slipper chairs, are restrained. The curtains are in a blush-toned sheer wool that filters the incoming light, lending the space a hushed, dreamlike atmosphere.

The two threads come together in the upstairs drawing room, where the walls are painted an old white that contrasts with the vibrant goldenrod of the upholstery and the custom-stamped gold border of the curtains, which are in a silk velvet by Sabina Fay Braxton. The goldenrod shade repeats throughout the home, such as in the velvet upholstery of the slipper chairs in a guest bedroom in the carriage house, where the warm hue engages in a funky dialogue with the zebra hide that covers the stark wood floor.

In a home of this age and pedigree, the biggest surprise is the ultramodern kitchen, with its minimalist European cabinetry, gray stone floors, and stainless-steel appliances. It is located on the first floor of the main house in what used to be the rear porch. I love the contrast between this contemporary and functional space in a historic setting. For me, the ideal project keeps one foot in the past and one in the present.

Right: Apricot silk lines the walls of the entry foyer, with curtains to match. The small space features an antique Oushak carpet, Empire chandelier, and a pair of Regency gilt-wood and caned chairs.
Following spread: The morning room gets its name from the quality of the light which streams into the space early in the day. The eclectic furnishings span three centuries, from the eighteenth-century Venetian sofa and candle sconces to the midcentury T. H. Robsjohn-Gibbings slipper chairs and a contemporary Lucite waterfall table.

Opposite: **An antique German ancestral portrait hangs on the walls, which received a sienna glaze for added depth.**

Above: **The Italian demilune pier table in the dining room is framed by chairs in Fortuny slipcovers. The chandelier is Empire.**

Right: To make the butler's panty feel more special, I covered the walls in hand-painted Gracie wallpaper. The serving table is English Regency. The chandelier is a converted Argand fixture.

Above: The rear porches of the house were converted into a modern stainless-steel kitchen. The minimalist European cabinetry is by Bulthaup.

Opposite: Antique wood pilasters were applied to the walls in the kitchen, along with a trio of collage art panels by Charleston artist William Halsey.

Following spread: The upstairs drawing room has an intriguing mix of textures, from the goldenrod Christopher Hyland upholstery on the four Napoleon chairs to the suede cover on an eighteenth-century armchair. An antique Khotan rug sits on a carpet of seagrass.

Above: An antique gilt-wood candleholder in the shape of a dolphin (left). Artisanal details, such as a velvet pillow hand-embroidered in metallic thread, add a sense of luxe (right).

Above: **The velvet curtains in the drawing room are framed with a classical border that has been gilded and hand-stamped.**

Above: In the master bedroom, the canopy of the Regency four-poster bed is in raw silk with bronze cording.

Opposite: A Sabina Fay Braxton blue-and-bronze stamped velvet covers the wall behind the bed, while a Paula Rubino painting is strategically hung near the room's entry.

Above: **A white enamel bathtub with a burnished silver base is the focal point of the master bathroom.**

Opposite: **The master dressing room is furnished with a pair of eighteenth-century French fauteuils and a 1940s brushed-steel and brass chandelier.**

Above and opposite: **The property has a separate kitchen house, which was converted into guest quarters. The guest bedroom, which retains its original exposed beams and wood floors, has a four-post iron bed with sheer bed hangings, an antique zebra rug, and amelia, inc. slipper chairs.**

Above and opposite: **The bathroom in the guest house has a glassed-in shower and working fireplace. A custom designed tall mirror with antiqued glass and a pleated-silk vanity skirt dress up the room.**

Manhattan Pied-à-Terre

*Upper East Side Apartment
Overlooking Central Park*

With an adventurous client and careful planning, a small apartment can be a showstopper. This two-room Manhattan pied-à-terre overlooking Central Park belongs to an author and former media executive. I had previously collaborated with her on two other houses—one on Charleston's Rainbow Row and a second home in the Hamptons. Her red drawing room in Charleston was a hit and she asked me to create a similar atmosphere in her compact prewar apartment on Fifth Avenue.

Located at ground level, the apartment largely consisted of a living room and a master bedroom, both with fourteen-foot ceilings. There was also a small hallway and an extremely compact kitchen, which sufficed since the building is one of just a handful left in Manhattan with a full-service dining room that can provide meals or even cater parties. This arrangement suits my client, who loves to entertain and thinks nothing of hosting eighteen people here for cocktails.

Getting the red right was the first order of business. Kristen Bunting, a decorative artist from Charleston, was drafted to customize the perfect shade of Venetian plaster for the living room walls. The challenge was to develop a hue that would complement the fabrics without overwhelming the small space. We concocted a rich berry hue that shifts from red to pink depending on the light and time of day. As in Charleston, we covered the ceiling in gold-leaf tea paper. Here, the gilded surface helps to create a glow in a room that does not receive much direct light.

In a small space, a few strategic architectural changes can make all the difference. The bedroom's entrance was shifted from the front hallway to a larger opening centered onto the living room. I had a set of jack-wood screens from India made into sliding doors to separate the two rooms. Even when the doors are closed, the perforated panels allow light into the living room from the bedroom, giving the space a more expansive feeling.

The salonlike living area was designed for maximum seating, from the ample red sofa by the window to the dramatic corner banquette covered in hand-stamped and gilded velvet and embellished with

Opposite: **The living room's red and gold palette was inspired by the homeowner's drawing room in Charleston.** *Above:* **On the sofa, cushions in vintage Fortuny fabric.**

Following spread: **A six-panel antique French painted screen was split in two and hung on the living room wall.**

an elaborate bullion passementerie trim. An open bookcase was refitted with antique-mirrored cabinet doors. A faux fireplace was removed and replaced with an antique pier table that serves as a bar. Behind it, I hung a tall gilt mirror that I designed with moldings wide enough to hold shaded sconce lights.

The master bedroom is no less rich, with its floor-to-ceiling bed canopy, tufted headboard, and gold tea-leaf walls. The curtains, from the Italian artist Mirella Spinella, are the genesis for the room's palette,

which ranges from copper to sage and turquoise. For new built-in closets, I designed doors inspired by the shape of a window I had once seen on a palazzo in Venice and had them painted and decorated to blend with the tea paper on the walls.

The grandeur of this small space, filled with dramatic color and overscaled furnishings, violates conventional design wisdom. The marriage of form, function, and texture in this jewel-box apartment makes it work.

Above: **In the master bedroom, the custom curtain fabric is by Venetian artist Mirella Spinella. The walls are covered in gold tea-leaf paper.**

Opposite: **A tufted headboard and bed canopy in velvet. The Japanese red lacquer tables are circa 1950.**

Rose Hill

*A Virginia
Plantation House*

Restoring the glory of a historical home with a venerable history brings me great satisfaction. Rose Hill stands as one of the most remarkable projects I've had the good fortune to participate in. John Hipkins built this magnificent house, which is situated on thirty acres in Virginia's beautiful Rappahannock River Valley, in 1790 as a simple two-story structure. His grandson, John Hipkins Bernard, who married a descendent of Pocahontas, later added a library, office, and a skylit music room. Remaining in the same family for generations, the house was updated in 1934 to include the addition of statuary and a very fine Dufour et Leroy wallpaper depicting scenes of Italy. Unfortunately,

a fire in 1959 destroyed much of the house, which was then partially rebuilt, but not in harmony with its historic materials or proportions.

The current owners are devotees of period architecture who loved the rolling Virginia landscape and recognized in Rose Hill an unpolished jewel of a house lurking beneath the dust. After consulting with a historian, they purchased the estate and began the formidable tasks of preservation and restoration. Original builder's invoices and old photographs were assembled, which proved indispensable in re-creating everything from marble mantels to moldings.

The owners retained Frederick Ecker II of Tidewater Preservation to plan the restoration and construction. I was invited to assist with the design of the new kitchen, bathrooms, and second-floor guest rooms, in addition to the decoration of the full interior. Fortunately, some of the original furnishings, including a harp, a rosewood pianoforte, beds, and a fantastic collection of small antique books, survived

Opposite: **An antique plaster bust of Napoleon rests on a bracket on the front porch. The new custom windows were double hung, weighted, and fitted with restoration glass.**

Above: **Rose Hill, an eighteenth-century house in Virginia, before the restoration (bottom) and after (top).**

145

Above: **The entry hall was painted in Benjamin Moore's Yorkshire Tan and furnished with a gilt-wood mirror original to the house and circa-1830 side chairs.**

Opposite: **The center hall is framed by four antique Baltimore classical side chairs, a prized set that once belonged to the Baltimore Museum of Art.**

Above: **Saffron curtains trimmed with tassels glow against the sand-colored walls.**
Opposite: **The yellow music room has a painted floor in tan and cream that echoes the palette in the center hall. The harp and piano date from the home's early years.**

Following spread: **The library was fitted with shelves to hold leather-bound books that have belonged to the house for nearly two centuries.**

Above: **The bookshelves frame a conversation nook.**
Opposite: **A late-eighteenth-century portrait of a Virginia lady hangs above the library's mantel.**

Following spread: **The dining room's walls are covered in Dufour et Leroy's circa-1822 grisaille wallpaper Vues d'Italie. The antique American dining table once hosted Confederate generals Robert E. Lee and J. E. B. Stuart.**

the fire in the home's basement. A fine Early American painted bench, found intact in its original upholstery, now graces the entry hall. Other items were reunited with the house through the Association for the Preservation of Virginia Antiquities.

Having these reclaimed treasures to integrate back into the house, my aim was to fill in the gaps and create a livable environment without detracting from its essential beauty. In the library, I designed a wall of classical bookshelves for the antique leather-bound volumes. The octagonal music room required equally remarkable flooring. Kristen Bunting, a decorative finish artist, was commissioned for the task of painting the floor. She applied an eighteenth-century geometric design that was central to establishing the room's graceful symmetry.

Above: A vintage image of the dining room's mantel. *Right:* The new custom mantel is topped by an eighteenth-century portrait of a Virginia gentleman. The large circa-1819 server and cabinet is attributed to Chester Sully, a brother of the portrait painter Thomas Sully.

Above: The kitchen blends into its surroundings with paneled cabinetry and a marble-topped island with an antique wood shelf.

Opposite: The mudroom has diamond-patterned painted floors and a contemporary globe from Robert Long Lighting. The homeowners' collection of cow prints hangs on the wall.

Above: **A guest suite has a soothing monochromatic cream palette, from the laurel-wreath wallpaper to the scalloped half-corona bed crown and upholstered headboard.**

Opposite: **An antique portrait hangs over an English Regency settee.**

The overall color scheme consists mainly of neutrals. To create richness, we layered bolder fabrics on this subdued palette. Even in the monochromatic guest room, for example, multiple textures abound—from the laurel-wreath patterned wallpaper to the damask upholstery of the skirted chairs.

The dining room is a remarkable space. Although the original 1934 French wallpaper had been destroyed in the fire, it had been replaced with an identical replica that now had to be painstakingly protected on its plaster walls while the upper part of the house was temporarily removed. The grisaille imagery, block-printed to resemble an etching, depicts the Bay of Naples with an ever-threatening Mount Vesuvius smoking in the distance.

Today, Rose Hill provides a visitor with the experience of walking through an eighteenth-century Virginia plantation, with house, grounds, and garden as originally conceived. For me, the project demanded a lot of restraint, and ultimately, that I learn to trust in the value of that which is original.

Above: **Another guest room, painted gold, has a circa-1830 mahogany American four-poster bed. The screen is covered in a vintage Fortuny fabric. The custom chair, in a Rose Tarlow chinoiserie linen, has a scalloped skirt.**

Opposite: **A sitting area in the former kitchen house, which is now a guest cottage.**

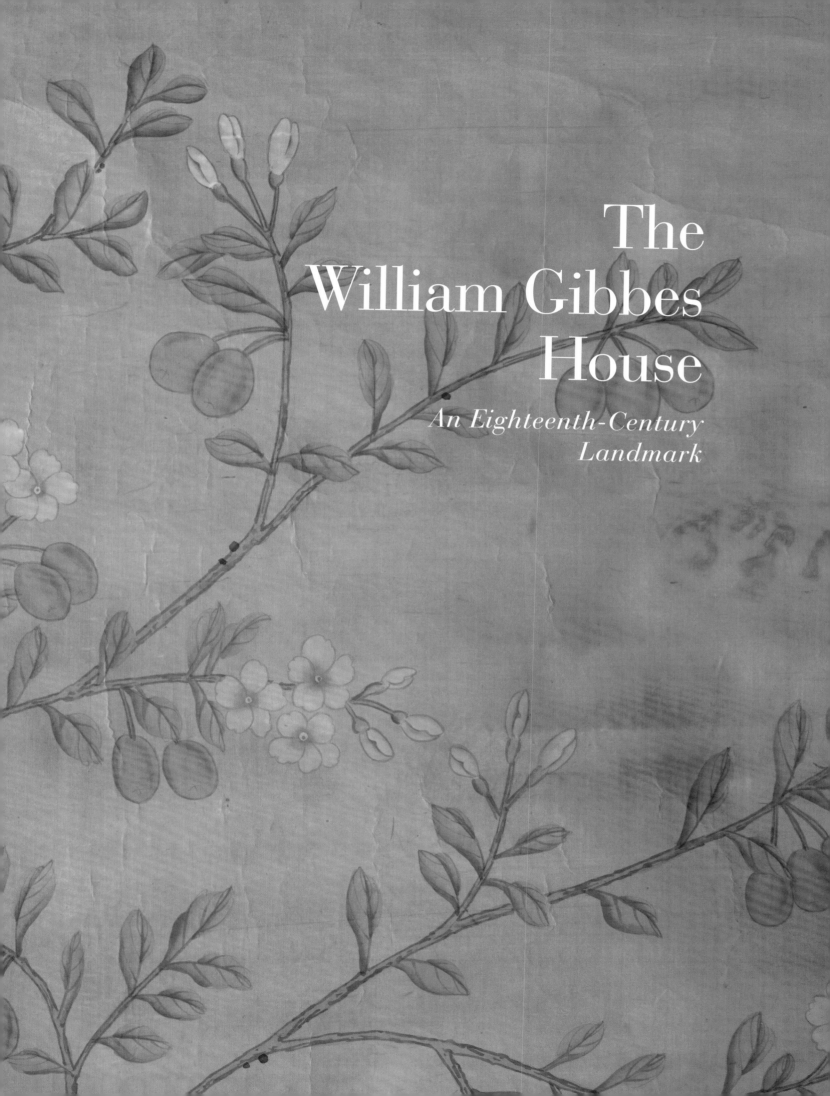

The
William Gibbes
House

An Eighteenth-Century
Landmark

Set on the north side of Charleston's South Battery, the 1772 William Gibbes House is one of the oldest and most architecturally significant homes in town. The Georgian-style painted wood-frame house was constructed by Gibbes, a wealthy ship owner and merchant.

The property was almost sold in the 1980s to a developer who planned to build condominiums in its historic garden but the Historic Charleston Foundation interceded. It purchased the national historic landmark, restored the property, and began a search for preservation-minded buyers. My client acquired the house in 1986. Ten years later, she and her husband invited me to join in on the adventure of the redecoration of the landmark house.

The home's rooms reflect a wonderful history, with Georgian details blending with Adamesque features, such as plaster medallions, carved mantels, and corner fans, that were likely added in a 1794 restyling. In 1928, the home was extensively modernized by Cornelia Roebling, a widow of one of the builders of the Brooklyn Bridge. The new owner took the advice of the foundation and restored the layout of the interior to its original Georgian floor plan, which now follows the flow of a classic Charleston double house. There are four rooms on each floor, including two on each side of a majestic central hall that rises above the home's curving staircase with its wrought-iron railing.

The architectural restoration was complete by the time I became involved. The dining room had been returned to its original square dimension. What was once a large pantry behind the kitchen was now a more convenient kitchen than the large basement kitchen that had existed during Mrs. Roebling's time in the house. I helped to refine the kitchen and breakfast room and redid the master bath and dressing room. Other than those areas, the house largely remained as it looked when it was purchased.

I encouraged the couple to retain some of Mrs. Roebling's more elegant improvements. We were fortunate that the central hall retained its panoramic wallpaper from the legendary French firm Zuber. The pattern, with its moody sky and lush foliage, adds visual interest to the large space. The library still had its chinoiserie silk wall covering of birds and flowers. Upstairs, the 1928 chandelier

Opposite: **The entry hall catches the morning sun.**

Above: **The 1772 William Gibbes House in Charleston.**

167

that Mrs. Roebling commissioned from Tiffany still glitters in the ballroom.

I took my color cues from the Zuber wall covering, which features a range of hues that had been muted by the patina of time. The wallpaper's shades—soft greens that blend into blues, multiple shades of gold, and accents of red—made their way around the home's first floor.

When working on the interiors of an older home, I'm always conscious of finding a balance between respecting the past and creating an environment that works for today. In this case, the house itself dictated these moves. For instance, in the sitting room, the exuberant wallpaper called for fabric that matched its energy. The sofa and chairs were covered in a tomato red shade found in the flowers on the silk paper. The blue-green silk curtains have the smallest bit of the same "not-quite-red," which has a touch of orange in it, at the top. A French chair upholstered in a silk jaguar pattern adds to the eclectic atmosphere of the room. In the dining room, we went all out with red walls, wool sheers with gold trim, and red-and-gold Fortuny slipcovers on the dining chairs.

We experimented with a range of color possibilities for the ballroom, but somehow the original hue, a medium-toned purple brown, always seemed the most fitting and original, so we kept it. I designed four large chairs so the room could be used for conversation after dinner. The seats have a streamlined appearance, which feels up to date, while the gold silk slipcovers lend a touch of splendor, which feels right in the grand space. The mirrored table was designed for glamour but also to hold the group together. It is a version of the table seen in the eighteenth-century portrait above the fireplace.

Right: **A previous owner had installed the panoramic wallpaper from the French firm Zuber. We added a circa-1800 English tall case clock and a pair of Italian benches (one of which is visible here) with gilt-wood legs and tobacco silk upholstery.**

Above: A portrait of the homeowner hangs on the paneled fireplace wall in the sitting room.

Opposite: The walls have a hand-painted silk wall covering. Upholstered furniture in red damask linen contrasts with the jaguar-patterned velvet on a French armchair.

In a home with such a rich palette, it's nice to give the eye a rest. For this reason, the master bedroom was kept light and bright. The walls were painted three shades of cream for interest. The combination of tones allowed the paneling to be shaded for depth. The windows were dressed in the simplest of silk damask sheers. The woven cane bed was repainted with a taupe and gold finish.

The owners enjoyed collecting art and antiques for the house. Many of the best pieces were found right here in Charleston, including the British tall case clock that is placed in the entry hall and the circa-1810 Philadelphia sideboard in the dining room.

Left: **The intact ballroom retained its decorative plaster ceiling and 1928 Tiffany chandelier. I designed four large-scale chairs with silk taffeta slipcovers for a conversation area.**
Above: **A vintage photograph of the home's ballroom.**

Above: **The master bedroom has a calming palette of cream and natural tones. The antique woven cane bed was refinished in taupe and gold.**

Opposite: **A richly carved Adamesque door casing leads into the master bedroom.**

Nineteenth-Century House

An Elegant Home in Town

When the owners of the William Gibbes House called to tell me they were selling their house and downsizing to a much smaller one on nearby King Street, I have to confess that my heart skipped a beat. As a decorator, I can't help but become attached to my projects. I couldn't imagine them living anywhere else. But with only the two of them at home they no longer needed such a large house. The move made sense for them and I, of course, unhesitatingly agreed to help with the interior design.

The brick house was a century newer than their former house, but it came with its own brand of charm. The home is laid out around a courtyard, which brings natural light into the common areas. And although there is no space here as grand as a ballroom, the rooms have elegant proportions and some wonderful details such as the antique English pine mantel and matching paneling in the library.

The couple had acquired a rich collection of antiques, fine furnishings, lighting, and artwork for their former home. The difficulty was in choosing what to keep. The decision-making process was challenging, but when it worked, it was invigorating. Objects that had seemed inseparable from their previous space now had fresh appeal in their new one. For instance, three pieces culled from the former ballroom— a pair of gilt mirrors and an eighteenth-century painting—now became the focal point of a small receiving room. The dining room, while nowhere near as large as the one in their last house, accommodated an antique Philadelphia sideboard and their collection of Chinese export porcelain.

When possible, I use furnishings that feel collected over time. In this case, the process was natural since the owners had traveled extensively and acquired many things of special significance—from the antique English rosewood dining table to a pair of eighteenth-century French portraits, which they had purchased in Provence. The new house now relies on an eclectic mix, which is grounded by the gray blue in the foyer and dining room and the gold in the drawing room. The window treatments—long

Opposite: **A pair of antique Italian chairs with a dolphin motif greets visitors in the entry hall.**

Above: **The house on King Street in Charleston.**

curtains that hang from bronze-finished iron rods—are the height of simplicity.

Many of the family's furnishings would simply not fit in the new rooms, but we made a special effort to use anything to which they had become especially attached. When they balked at giving up the huge Aubusson rug that had graced the former ballroom, we made the difficult choice to cut it to fit the master bedroom. The carpet's trimmings were fashioned into a hall rug.

Previous spread: **The homeowners, who had lived in the William Gibbes House (see previous chapter), had a sizable collection of art and furniture. We moved an antique portrait and a pair of antique mirrors from the old ballroom into the entry hall of their new home.**
Right: **The drawing room, painted a vibrant gold, has an eighteenth-century chinoiserie secretary.**
Following spread: **The drawing room has a custom mohair sofa and a mirrored cocktail table with carved hoof feet. The carpet is an antique Oushak.**

Right: In the dining room, a circa-1810 Philadelphia sideboard holds the homeowners' collection of antique silver and blue-and-white Chinese export porcelain.
Following spread: The library, with English antique pine paneling and mantel, has casual slipcovered upholstered furniture.

Historic City House

A Late Eighteenth-Century Brick Home

Decorating a home is a process that can involve countless decisions, but if you are fortunate the house itself will show you the way. I have found this to be true of most well-preserved historic homes, and it was certainly the case when I was asked to design interiors for a 1770 single house in Charleston. The previous owner, who had lived there since the 1950s, was an antiques collector. As part of the purchase agreement, my clients were granted first right of refusal on the house's contents.

I was hired for the project along with the architect Randolph Martz. There were numerous wonderful pieces in the house and the first step was to decide what furnishings were to stay. We kept the dining room's sconces and chandelier as well as a pier table that dated back to an even earlier owner. There was a Venetian sofa and a set of gilded curtain rods that were perfect in the drawing room. Last but not least was an Aubusson rug, whose soft palette became a font of color inspiration for the project. Soft blues and greens with a hint of pink became dominant hues for the house. A tobacco brown was then used to temper the pastels.

Before we could start painting the walls, the brick house had to undergo a substantial restoration and renovation. In fact, it had scarcely been altered since the nineteenth century, with the exception of an outbuilding that had been converted in the 1940s to an artist's studio. Randolph updated the nine-over-nine windows with hand-blown restoration glass and converted the artist's studio into a loftlike modern kitchen with stainless-steel appliances and vintage industrial bar stools. Throughout the house, plaster walls were repaired and painted, wide-plank floors were waxed, and ceiling beams were uncovered and cleaned.

The homeowners were intent on preserving the existing character of their house but did not want intimidating period interiors. To that end, we mixed furniture and art from different periods. In the living room, for example, a nineteenth-century artwork by the American portrait painter Thomas Sully hangs over the mantel, while an eighteenth-century Venetian sofa is flanked by Swedish Rococo chairs. I designed a set of high-backed slipper chairs for a conversation area near

Opposite: **A painting by Stephanus Heidacker hangs over a rustic trestle table.**

Above: **The Charleston single house, built in 1770.**

Above and opposite: The set of elaborate antique gilt curtain poles with ornately carved finials in the living room are from the former owner. I designed a group of slipper chairs for the room, which also has a 1940s Italian églomisé cocktail table and an eighteenth-century Venetian sofa.

Opposite: **The loftlike kitchen is located in what was once a separate artist's studio and is now connected to the main house. The kitchen island has an antique-board shelf and a marble top.**

Above: **Artwork is hung salon–style in the stair hall.**

the fireplace. For ambiance, the chandelier is lit with candles. Meanwhile, in the master bedroom, a Regency four-poster looks almost modernist when stripped of its canopy, and simply covered in white linens and a throw made out of a blue-and-gold silk sari.

The goal was to keep the interiors feeling light and never overdone. Windows were dressed simply; upholstery was generally in quieter tones. Look closer, though, and the devil was in the details, from the dressmaker's finishes like smocked headings on curtains and pleated skirts on slipcovers.

Right: **A Regency four-poster bed with a blue-painted tester is covered in a silk sari in the master bedroom. The windows have antique French embroidered valances.**
Following spread: **An upstairs guest bathroom was painted in a stenciled pattern.**

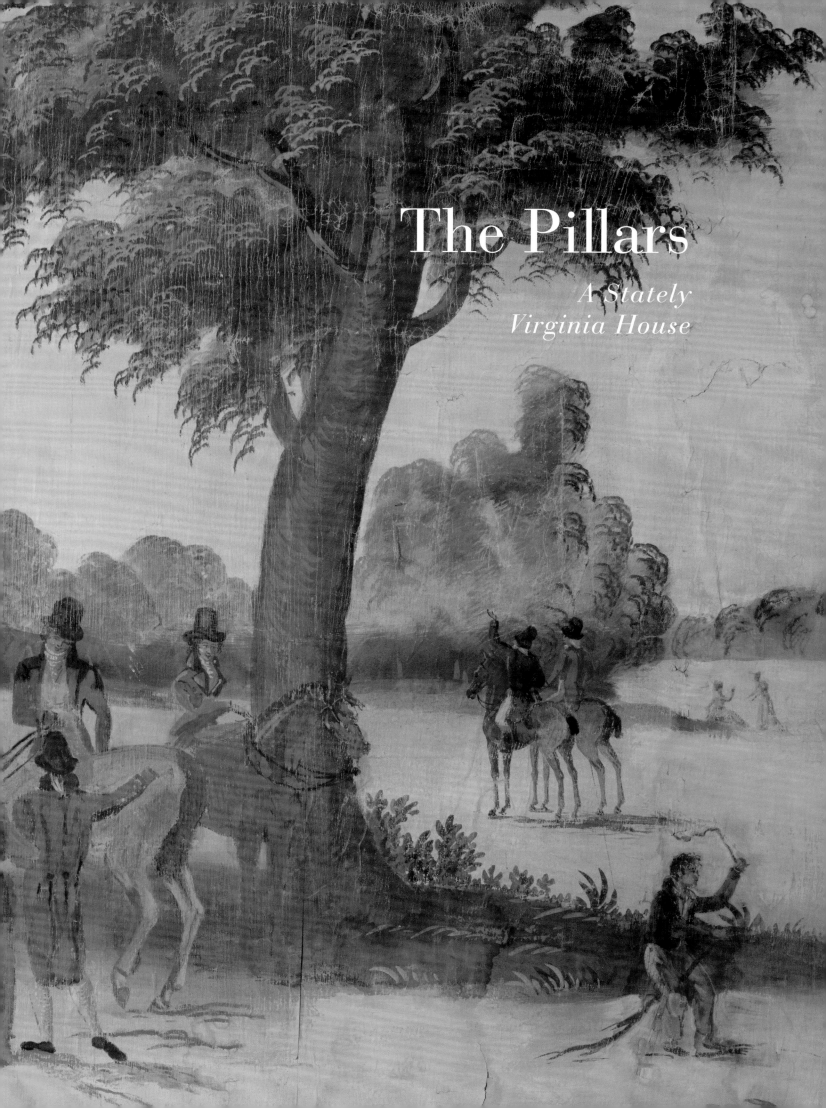

The Pillars

*A Stately
Virginia House*

The village of Hot Springs, Virginia, tucked away in the Blue Ridge Mountains, has long attracted visitors drawn to cool summer nights, clean air, and therapeutic waters. The Pillars, a large Greek Revival, is one of a handful of grand homes built in the late nineteenth century in this historic spa town.

With commanding views from its hilltop position, the house, with an impressive white columned façade and wide verandas, has hosted a noteworthy list of summer visitors including Thomas Edison and Grover Cleveland. When acquired by its present owners, the structure was in need of care, caused in part by a fire that had destroyed much of the upper house.

Reclaiming the Pillars' former glory would prove a formidable task. The homeowners retained the classical architect Allan Greenberg to oversee the renovation, beginning with the temporary removal of the home's signature pillars, which permitted reconstruction of the fire-damaged roof and surrounding structures. When the exterior work was complete, the central hallway staircase received new detail work that blended seamlessly with the original architecture. The exterior was repainted in gleaming white except for the portico ceilings, which called for a traditional sky blue.

I chose to keep the interior pale as well, but upon close inspection one will find over twenty distinct paint colors used in the house. The catalyst for all of these shades is the Robert Kime faded linen print used in the living room curtains. It contains beautifully nuanced colors that inspired a range of diverse paint choices such as the choice of Farrow & Ball's Dutch Pink for the dining room. This hue is a particular favorite of mine for its ability to run the color gamut of appearance throughout the day, ranging from apricot to deep rose depending on the available slant of light. Those curtains also foreshadowed the use of several shades of gray and lavender in a guest room.

When an interior color palette springs from a unifying source, such as a painting or textile, I will often draw from its less obvious elements. So while the living room's wheat walls were clearly

Opposite: **The home's original oak floors were dressed up with a hand-stenciled pattern.**

Above: **The Pillars' Greek Revival façade in Virginia.**

inspired by those curtains, so too was the blue gray that I selected for the stairway hall. In this way, the colors flow harmoniously, layer upon layer throughout the house, as they did in the fabric that originally inspired their selection.

For the Pillars, those linen curtains were also chosen because they evoked the ease of summer. Their straightforward textural simplicity mixes beautifully with a range of textiles, including silks, damasks, and crewels. Sumptuous Fortuny pillows follow suit and complete the picture. So while the living room's interior is undeniably luxurious, the overall feeling is one of refined relaxation.

Even in a historic home, I try to avoid using furnishings of only one style or era. Here, for example, we layered a combination of antiques from diverse temporal and geographic origins. The dining room, where a late-nineteenth-century French crystal chandelier illuminates an 1820s English mahogany table, illustrates these crosscurrents. Underfoot is an early-twentieth-century Turkish Oushak carpet. The Pillars' interior illustrates that a classical structure can accommodate a range of furnishings without looking contrived or confused.

Right: **The dining room is painted in one of my favorite colors, Farrow & Ball's Dutch Pink, which has a warm glow in the evening. The mahogany table is English Regency.**

Above: The palette in the living room was inspired by the faded coral of the Robert Kime linen curtain fabric.
Opposite: A custom sofa in a faded red velvet sits below a hand-painted panel depicting pastoral scenes.

Following spread: An abaca rug and linen fabrics lighten the atmosphere in the living room.

Above: In the kitchen, a stainless-steel range and hood add an industrial counterpoint to a room furnished with antiques.

Opposite: The butler's pantry has patterned wallpaper and a Roman shade in hemp linen.

Above: In the master bedroom, a pair of damask-covered chairs frames a nineteenth-century ottoman with its original needlepoint cover. The four-poster bed is reproduction Chippendale.

Opposite: A guest bedroom has pale taupe walls and window treatments in a Robert Kime lavender-and-green linen floral. The antique painted commode is Dutch.

Above: **A circa-1820 églomisé mirror with an image of George Washington hangs in the entry hall above an English Regency side table.**

Opposite: **Floral throw pillows add a touch of comfort to the outdoor wicker furniture on the front porch.**

The Studio

The heart of our design office is a studio on the ground floor of the former McCrory's five-and-dime on Upper King Street in Charleston. When I moved my studio into the space a decade ago, the city was just beginning to recast the historic neighborhood—which dates back to the Civil War and boomed as a shopping district in the 1940s and 1950s—as Charleston's new "design district." I was drawn to this enclave filled with classic old retailers like Read Brothers, a notions store that still sells fabric, thread, and clothing. I have patronized the shop since my college days, when I used to go there to buy Indian bedspreads, beads, and textiles. I still can't resist walking in there.

Several new design-oriented businesses have helped transform the area around Upper King Street into Charleston's "Soho." Boutique hotels and fashionable restaurants coexist here alongside furniture shops and cocktail lounges. I do enjoy the neighborhood's renaissance but admit to feeling a twinge of loss whenever one of the older businesses is replaced with something new.

When I initiate a new project, I encourage clients to visit our studio and showroom. Our soaring space is the back of the former five-and-dime, now divided into two levels. The main floor serves as a showroom for the upholstered furniture I design, as well as accessories, textiles, and art. Glass doors fold back to open onto our conference room where an old Belgian jewelers table is used for meetings.

Our work spaces are on the upper level along with an ever-expanding design library. Charleston is filled with wonderful antiques shops and artisans, but we don't have a professional design center in town. Fortunately, we are able to obtain samples from representatives of many of the best showrooms in the nation. In our library, we maintain thousands of swatches of fabrics, trimmings, and rugs, sorted into specific categories ranging from small prints to damasks to florals and stripes. Our samples run the gamut from the most basic canvas and duck fabrics to the most luxurious velvets and hand-embroidered silks.

For me, designing an interior rarely takes a linear path. We begin with detailed drawings of a space, down to the placement of walls, doors, and electrical layouts. From there, we create a design plan for the dominant elements, such as colors and furnishings, for key areas of the home. The color palette informs the project going forward, but also allows for flexibility and layering as things progress. Every project incorporates some element of handmade craft. We tap into our extensive network of specialized artisans, a list that includes upholsterers, plasterers, floor painters, and blacksmiths. We carefully explain to clients how their skills can enhance their projects.

While the Internet has undeniably become an important tool in product selection, no online image can compare with being able to see and touch objects and materials in person. In my experience, those who are willing (and patient) enough to participate in the unfolding of this process in the early stages often derive immense satisfaction in the end results.

Left: **The studio's conference room is furnished with an antique table and Chinese chairs. Our design offices are located behind the glass wall on the upper floor.**

Resources

INTERIORS

FURNISHINGS

amelia, inc.
athid.com

Billy Baldwin Studio
billybaldwinstudio.com

David Duncan Antiques
davidduncanantiques.com

David Skinner Antiques and Period Lighting
davidskinnerantiques.com

English Accent Antiques
englishaccentantiques.com

G. Sergeant Antiques
gsergeant.com

Golden and Associates
goldenassociatesantiques.com

Max Rollitt
maxrollitt.com

Niall Smith Antiques
niallsmithantiques@gmail.com

O'Sullivan Antiques
osullivanantiques.com

Parc Monceau Antiques Ltd.
parcmonceau.com

Robuck
robuck.com

William Word Fine Antiques
williamwordantiques.com

TEXTILES

B. Viz Design
www.bviz.com

Fortuny
fortuny.com

Holland and Sherry
hollandsherry.com

Julia B. Couture Linens
juliab.com

Loro Piana
loropiana.com

Mirella Spinella
mirellaspinella.com

Rosemary Hallgarten
rosemaryhallgarten.com

Sabina Fay Braxton
sabinafaybraxton.com

WALLCOVERING

Gracie
graciestudio.com

Maya Romanoff
mayaromanoff.com

Phillip Jeffries
phillipjeffries.com

Roger Arlington
rogerarlington.com

Weitzner Limited
weitznerlimited.com

CARPETS

Galerie Shabab
galerieshabab.com

Keivan Woven Arts
keivanwovenarts.com

Sullivan Fine Rugs
sulllivanfinerugs.com

LIGHTING

Charles Edwards
charlesedwards.com

Edgar Reeves
edgar-reeves.com

Jamb
jamb.co.uk

Marvin Alexander
marvinalexander.com

Robert Long Lighting
robertlonglighting.com

Urban Electric Co.
urbanelectricco.com

WORKROOMS

O'Kelly's Upholstery
okelleysupholstery.com

Virginia's Sewing Workshop
virginiaspc@hotmail.com

Willard Pitt Curtain Makers
willardpittcurtainmakers.com

ARCHITECTS

Allan Greenberg Architect
allangreenberg.com

Beau Clowney Architects
beauclowney.com

Fairfax & Sammons
fairfaxandsammons.com

Glenn Keyes Architects
glennkeyesarchitects.com

Randolph Martz
randolphmartz.com

Stumphouse Architecture + Design
stumphouse.com

ARCHITECTURAL CONSERVATION

Richard Marks Restorations, Inc.
richardmarksrestorations.com

Tidewater Preservation Inc.
tidewaterpreservation.com

LANDSCAPE ARCHITECTS

Preservation Green LLC
preservationgreenllc.com

Rieley & Associates
rieleyandassociates.com

Wertimer and Associates
wertimer.com

ARTISTS AND ARTISANS

Hines Studio Ltd.
oldmirrorglass.com

Kristen Bunting
kristenbunting@comcast.net

Nietert Antique Restoration
bnietert@gmail.com

Raymond Goins
rlgoins.com

Scott Waterman
scottwatermanartist.com

Timothy McDowell
timothymcdowell.format.com

Todd Murphy
toddmurphy.com

GALLERIES

Ann Long Fine Art
annlongfineart.com

Tew Galleries
tewgalleries.com

Opposite: **A Pichwai painting from India hangs behind an Anglo-Indian rosewood desk, which holds an arrangement of objects including a bronze Buddha, Indian silver, Sheffield hurricanes, and a Chinese incense burner with red lacquer.**
Above: **A lacquered bedside table holds purple bottles and an antique Tibetan horn made into a lamp. The painting is by Donald Sutphin.**

Acknowledgments

I would like to thank the following people who
helped make this book possible:

Pieter Estersohn, who not only captured these rooms
in beautiful repose, but also
encouraged me to do this book.

Ingrid Abramovitch, who showed skillful patience
working with a nonverbal procrastinator.

Sandy Gilbert Freidus, whose guiding hand
ultimately brought this project to reality.

Gil Shuler, who maintained both a sense of humor
and his sharp eye for great graphic style throughout.

The designers at ATHID, who offered their creativity,
and especially Gil Evans, who worked diligently to
maintain a bit of order and sanity.

Sabina Fay Braxton, for her friendship and great
artistry and for allowing her sumptuous textiles to
find their way onto many of these pages.

And Leonard Cohen,
who reminds us how the light gets in.

Opposite: **A detail of an early-nineteenth-century Italian
leather screen.**

223

First published in the United States of America in 2016
by Rizzoli International Publications, Inc.
300 Park Avenue South
New York, New York 10010
www.rizzoliusa.com

Text © 2016 by Amelia Handegan

Principal photography © 2016 by Pieter Estersohn

All photography by Pieter Estersohn with the exception of
the following images:
J. Savage Gibson: page 29
Tria Giovan: page 13
Amelia Handegan: pages 32–33, 42
Max Kim-Bee: pages 18–19, 21–27, 30–31, 204–217
Jeff McNamara: page 14
Eric Piasecki: pages 70–79
Rick Rhodes: pages 16, 52, 68, 80, 108, 134, 164, 190, 202, 222

Endpapers: Courtesy of Sabina Fay Braxton. Detail of textile
(Inferno color no. 08 Lentille with multi inking)

Published with permission from:

Architectural Digest
Fish and Goat: pages 34–39, 41, 43, 45, 46–49. First published July 2011
Rose Hill: pages 144, 146–147, 149–151, 153–155, 158, 160. First published June 2013

Southern Accents Style Guide
Island Home: pages 70–73, 75, 77–79

Veranda
Birdsong: pages 19, 21–26, 30–31. First published September/October 2014
The Pillars: pages 204–207, 210–213, 217. First published August 2013

All rights reserved. No part of this publication may be reproduced, stored in
a retrieval system, or transmitted in any form or by any means, electronic,
mechanical, photocopying, recording, or otherwise, without prior consent of
the publisher.

Project Editor: Sandra Gilbert
Art Direction: Gil Shuler Graphic Design, Inc.
Production Manager: Susan Lynch

2016 2017 2018 2019 / 10 9 8 7 6 5 4 3 2 1

Printed in China

ISBN-13: 978-0-8478-4930-7

Library of Congress Control Number: 201693909

Page 1: Detail of a bodice on an eighteenth-century painting.
Above: Below an eighteenth-century French mirror, a Jamaican blanket chest
is topped with ivory candlesticks, a Chinese blanc de chine carved porcelain
bowl on a stand, and a lamp made from a gilded architectural fragment.